EMMANUEL JOSEPH

The Wellness Symphony, Orchestrating Financial Independence with Personal Flourishment

Copyright © 2025 by Emmanuel Joseph

All rights reserved. No part of this publication may be reproduced, stored or transmitted in any form or by any means, electronic, mechanical, photocopying, recording, scanning, or otherwise without written permission from the publisher. It is illegal to copy this book, post it to a website, or distribute it by any other means without permission.

First edition

This book was professionally typeset on Reedsy.
Find out more at reedsy.com

Contents

1. Chapter 1: The Prelude – Setting the Stage ... 1
2. Chapter 2: Understanding the Score – Financial Literacy... ... 3
3. Chapter 3: Composing Your Financial Plan ... 5
4. Chapter 4: The Harmony of Earnings – Maximizing Income... ... 7
5. Chapter 5: The Rhythm of Savings – Building a Secure Future ... 9
6. Chapter 6: The Crescendo of Investments – Growing Your... ... 11
7. Chapter 7: The Cadence of Debt Management – Eliminating... ... 13
8. Chapter 8: The Dynamics of Wealth Preservation – Protecting... ... 15
9. Chapter 9: The Symphony of Personal Flourishment –... ... 17
10. Chapter 10: The Ensemble of Support – Building a Strong... ... 19
11. Chapter 11: The Movement of Mindfulness – Embracing Present... ... 21
12. Chapter 12: The Melody of Giving – Embracing Generosity ... 23
13. Chapter 13: The Refrain of Resilience – Overcoming... ... 25
14. Chapter 14: The Opus of Legacy – Creating a Lasting Impact ... 27
15. Chapter 15: The Finale – Celebrating the Journey ... 29

1

Chapter 1: The Prelude – Setting the Stage

In the grand symphony of life, financial independence often plays the melody while personal fulfillment provides the harmony. To start on this harmonious journey, we must first recognize the importance of balance. It's not solely about amassing wealth, but about integrating financial stability with personal growth. The pursuit of money and well-being should not be at odds; instead, they can coalesce to create a fulfilling existence.

Understanding the role of financial literacy is crucial. Educating oneself about savings, investments, and smart spending lays a solid foundation. Financial independence begins with knowing how to manage money effectively, yet this must be accompanied by a keen sense of self-awareness. What drives you? What are your passions? These inquiries pave the way for setting realistic goals that align with both financial and personal aspirations.

Developing a symphony requires a well-thought-out plan, much like orchestrating a piece of music. Establishing short-term and long-term goals can be likened to composing different movements in a symphony. Each goal should resonate with your core values and contribute to the larger purpose of your life's composition. Remember, the ultimate objective is to create a harmonious blend where financial security and personal growth complement each other.

Finally, surround yourself with a supportive ensemble. This includes mentors, financial advisors, and like-minded individuals who can provide guidance and encouragement. Just as musicians rely on each other to bring out the best performance, you, too, can draw strength and wisdom from a well-chosen network.

2

Chapter 2: Understanding the Score – Financial Literacy Basics

Financial literacy forms the basic score upon which the symphony of wellness is built. Understanding key concepts such as budgeting, saving, and investing is fundamental. Just like reading music, one must become proficient in interpreting financial statements, comprehending interest rates, and recognizing the implications of debt.

A detailed budget acts as the sheet music for your financial composition. It outlines your income, expenses, and savings, ensuring that every financial note is accounted for. This practice helps in identifying areas where you can cut unnecessary costs and redirect funds towards meaningful investments. Saving, often seen as a tedious exercise, can be transformed into a rewarding endeavor by setting clear, achievable goals.

Investing is the crescendo in your financial symphony. It's where your money starts working for you, compounding over time to create wealth. Understanding different investment vehicles – stocks, bonds, real estate, mutual funds – is essential. Each instrument in this orchestra plays a unique role in building a diversified portfolio that mitigates risk while maximizing returns.

Finally, staying informed about financial trends and seeking continuous education helps in adapting to changing economic conditions. Much like how musicians practice regularly to refine their skills, maintaining and updating your financial knowledge ensures that you stay ahead and make informed decisions that align with your evolving goals.

3

Chapter 3: Composing Your Financial Plan

Composing a financial plan is akin to writing a symphony. It requires foresight, creativity, and meticulous attention to detail. Begin by assessing your current financial situation – your assets, liabilities, income, and expenses. This comprehensive overview serves as the overture, setting the tone for the rest of your financial journey.

Next, define your financial goals. These are the movements within your symphony, each with its distinct rhythm and melody. Short-term goals may include building an emergency fund or paying off credit card debt, while long-term goals could involve saving for retirement or purchasing a home. Ensure that these goals are Specific, Measurable, Achievable, Relevant, and Time-bound (SMART).

Creating a roadmap involves selecting the right financial instruments to achieve your goals. This is where understanding your risk tolerance and investment preferences comes into play. Diversification, like varying musical instruments in a symphony, ensures that your investments are balanced and resilient against market fluctuations.

Lastly, review and adjust your financial plan regularly. Life's circumstances change, and so should your financial strategies. Periodic assessments allow you to fine-tune your approach, ensuring that your financial symphony remains in harmony with your evolving personal and financial aspirations.

4

Chapter 4: The Harmony of Earnings – Maximizing Income Potential

Earnings are the melody that drives the financial symphony. Maximizing your income potential involves both enhancing your current earnings and creating additional streams of income. Begin by identifying opportunities for career advancement, whether through acquiring new skills, seeking promotions, or exploring new job opportunities that offer better compensation.

Entrepreneurship is another avenue for amplifying your income. Consider turning your passions and hobbies into profitable ventures. Whether it's freelancing, consulting, or starting a small business, the entrepreneurial path allows you to leverage your talents and interests for financial gain. Additionally, passive income streams, such as rental properties, dividend stocks, or royalties, provide a steady flow of earnings with minimal effort.

Investing in yourself is a crucial component of income maximization. Continuous learning and professional development enhance your skill set, making you more valuable in the job market. This, in turn, opens doors to higher-paying opportunities and positions of greater responsibility.

Finally, optimizing your financial decisions by minimizing taxes and managing expenses effectively ensures that more of your hard-earned money is retained and put to productive use. Seek professional advice to navigate the complexities of tax planning and take advantage of available deductions and credits.

5

Chapter 5: The Rhythm of Savings – Building a Secure Future

Savings form the steady rhythm that underpins the financial symphony, providing stability and security. Developing a disciplined savings habit ensures that you are prepared for unexpected expenses and future financial needs. Start by establishing an emergency fund that covers at least three to six months' worth of living expenses. This fund acts as a safety net, protecting you from financial setbacks.

Automate your savings to create a consistent and effortless saving routine. Setting up automatic transfers to your savings accounts ensures that a portion of your income is consistently set aside, reducing the temptation to spend impulsively. Additionally, consider opening multiple savings accounts for different goals, such as travel, education, or major purchases. This approach allows you to allocate funds specifically for each objective.

Take advantage of high-yield savings accounts and other low-risk investment options to grow your savings. While these may not offer substantial returns, they provide a secure place to store your money with minimal risk. Certificates of deposit (CDs) and money market accounts are also viable options for building a secure savings portfolio.

Finally, embrace the practice of mindful spending. This involves being intentional with your expenditures, prioritizing needs over wants, and finding ways to enjoy life without compromising your financial goals. Mindful spending ensures that your savings rhythm remains steady, supporting your journey towards financial independence.

6

Chapter 6: The Crescendo of Investments – Growing Your Wealth

Investing is the crescendo in your financial symphony, where your money starts to grow and compound over time. Begin by understanding the different types of investments available and how they align with your financial goals and risk tolerance. Stocks, bonds, real estate, mutual funds, and exchange-traded funds (ETFs) each offer unique opportunities and challenges.

Diversification is key to building a resilient investment portfolio. Just as a symphony features a variety of instruments, a well-diversified portfolio includes a mix of asset classes that balance risk and return. This approach minimizes the impact of market volatility on your overall investments, providing a smoother path to wealth accumulation.

Regularly review and rebalance your portfolio to ensure it remains aligned with your financial objectives. Market conditions and personal circumstances change over time, and your investment strategy should adapt accordingly. Rebalancing involves adjusting your asset allocation to maintain the desired level of risk and return.

Seek professional advice when needed to navigate the complexities of investing. Financial advisors can provide valuable insights and recommendations tailored to your specific situation. Additionally, stay informed about market trends and economic developments to make informed investment decisions that contribute to your financial crescendo.

7

Chapter 7: The Cadence of Debt Management – Eliminating Financial Burdens

Debt management is a crucial aspect of orchestrating financial independence. Just as a symphony requires precise timing and control, managing debt involves strategic planning and disciplined execution. Start by understanding the different types of debt you have, including credit card debt, student loans, mortgages, and personal loans. Prioritize paying off high-interest debt first, as it has the most significant impact on your financial health.

Develop a debt repayment plan that outlines the steps you need to take to eliminate your financial burdens. This plan should include a budget that allocates a specific portion of your income towards debt repayment. Consider using the snowball or avalanche method to pay off your debts systematically. The snowball method involves paying off smaller debts first to build momentum, while the avalanche method focuses on high-interest debts to minimize overall interest payments.

Refinancing and consolidating debt are additional strategies to consider. Refinancing involves obtaining a new loan with better terms to pay off existing debt, while consolidation combines multiple debts into a single loan with a lower interest rate. Both approaches can help reduce your monthly payments and simplify your debt management process.

Finally, avoid accumulating new debt by practicing mindful spending and living within your means. This involves prioritizing essential expenses, avoiding impulse purchases, and finding creative ways to enjoy life without overspending. By maintaining a disciplined approach to debt management, you can eliminate financial burdens and move closer to achieving financial independence.

8

Chapter 8: The Dynamics of Wealth Preservation – Protecting Your Assets

Wealth preservation is a vital component of financial independence, ensuring that your hard-earned assets are protected and continue to grow. Just as a symphony requires careful modulation of dynamics, wealth preservation involves implementing strategies to safeguard your financial future. Start by obtaining adequate insurance coverage to protect against unforeseen events. This includes health insurance, life insurance, disability insurance, and property insurance. Insurance provides a safety net that shields your assets from unexpected financial setbacks.

Estate planning is another critical aspect of wealth preservation. Develop a comprehensive estate plan that outlines how your assets will be managed and distributed in the event of your death or incapacitation.

This plan should include a will, power of attorney, and healthcare directives to ensure your wishes are honored and your assets are distributed according to your intentions. Additionally, consider setting up trusts to protect your assets from creditors and minimize estate taxes.

Tax planning is also essential for preserving wealth. Stay informed about tax laws and take advantage of deductions, credits, and other tax-saving strategies. Work with a tax professional to develop a comprehensive tax plan that minimizes your tax liability and maximizes your after-tax income. This proactive approach ensures that more of your wealth is preserved and available for future generations.

Regularly review your financial plan and make adjustments as needed. Life circumstances, market conditions, and personal goals can change over time, and your wealth preservation strategies should adapt accordingly. Periodic assessments ensure that your financial symphony remains in tune and continues to support your journey towards financial independence.

9

Chapter 9: The Symphony of Personal Flourishment – Cultivating Well-being

Personal flourishment is the harmony that complements financial independence, creating a balanced and fulfilling life. This involves nurturing your physical, mental, and emotional well-being to achieve a holistic sense of fulfillment. Start by prioritizing your health through regular exercise, a balanced diet, and sufficient sleep. Physical well-being provides the foundation for a vibrant and energetic life.

Mental well-being is equally important. Engage in activities that stimulate your mind and foster continuous learning. This could include reading, taking courses, or engaging in intellectually stimulating conversations. Cultivating a growth mindset and embracing lifelong learning enriches your life and opens new opportunities for personal and professional growth.

Emotional well-being involves building strong, supportive relationships and practicing self-care. Surround yourself with positive influences and engage in activities that bring joy and fulfillment. This could include hobbies, spending time with loved ones, or participating in community activities. Practicing mindfulness and stress management techniques, such as meditation or yoga, helps in maintaining emotional balance and resilience.

Ultimately, personal flourishment is about finding a sense of purpose and meaning in life. Reflect on your values, passions, and goals to identify what truly matters to you. Aligning your actions with your core values creates a sense of fulfillment and guides you towards a life of purpose and well-being.

10

Chapter 10: The Ensemble of Support – Building a Strong Network

A successful symphony requires a talented ensemble of musicians, and similarly, achieving financial independence and personal flourishment involves building a strong support network. Surrounding yourself with mentors, advisors, and like-minded individuals provides valuable guidance, encouragement, and accountability.

Seek out mentors who can offer insights and advice based on their own experiences. These individuals can provide valuable perspectives, help you navigate challenges, and offer encouragement as you work towards your goals. Building relationships with mentors involves being open to feedback, asking thoughtful questions, and showing gratitude for their support.

Financial advisors play a crucial role in your support network. These professionals can help you develop and implement a comprehensive financial plan, provide investment advice, and assist with tax planning. Working with a financial advisor ensures that you have expert guidance and support in making informed financial decisions.

Connecting with like-minded individuals who share your values and goals creates a sense of community and support. This could include joining professional organizations, attending networking events, or participating in online forums and groups. Engaging with a supportive community provides motivation, inspiration, and opportunities for collaboration.

Finally, nurture your personal relationships with family and friends. These connections provide emotional support, companionship, and a sense of belonging. Building strong personal relationships involves effective communication, empathy, and mutual respect.

11

Chapter 11: The Movement of Mindfulness – Embracing Present Awareness

Mindfulness is the practice of being present and fully engaged in the current moment. In the symphony of wellness, mindfulness serves as a guiding principle that enhances both financial independence and personal flourishment. Practicing mindfulness involves cultivating awareness of your thoughts, emotions, and surroundings, allowing you to respond to life's challenges with clarity and calm.

Start by incorporating mindfulness into your daily routine. This could involve setting aside time for meditation, practicing deep breathing exercises, or simply taking a few moments to be fully present in your activities. Mindfulness helps in reducing stress, improving focus, and enhancing overall well-being.

Mindful financial management involves being intentional with your spending and saving decisions. This means aligning your financial choices with your values and goals, and avoiding impulsive or emotionally-driven decisions. Practicing mindfulness in your financial life creates a sense of control and clarity, supporting your journey towards financial independence.

Incorporating mindfulness into your personal relationships enhances communication and connection. Being fully present in your interactions with others fosters deeper understanding and empathy. This practice strengthens your relationships and creates a sense of fulfillment and harmony in your personal life.

Overall, mindfulness is a powerful tool that enhances your ability to navigate life's challenges with grace and resilience. Embracing present awareness supports your journey towards financial independence and personal flourishment, creating a harmonious and fulfilling life.

12

Chapter 12: The Melody of Giving – Embracing Generosity

Generosity is a powerful melody that enriches the symphony of wellness. Embracing a mindset of giving not only benefits others but also brings a sense of fulfillment and purpose to your own life. Generosity can take many forms, from financial contributions to acts of kindness and volunteerism.

Start by identifying causes and organizations that align with your values and passions. Contributing to these causes provides a sense of purpose and connection to something larger than yourself. This could involve donating money, volunteering your time, or offering your skills and expertise to support a worthy cause.

Acts of kindness in your daily life also contribute to the melody of giving. Simple gestures, such as helping a neighbor, offering support to a friend, or showing appreciation to a colleague, create a positive impact and foster a sense of community and connection.

Consider integrating philanthropy into your financial plan. Setting aside a portion of your income for charitable contributions creates a structured approach to giving. This practice not only benefits others but also reinforces your commitment to making a positive impact in the world.

Finally, sharing your knowledge and experiences with others is a powerful way to give back. Mentoring, teaching, or simply offering advice and support to those in need creates a ripple effect of positive influence. Embracing generosity enhances your own sense of fulfillment and contributes to the harmony of your financial and personal life.

13

Chapter 13: The Refrain of Resilience – Overcoming Challenges

Resilience is the ability to adapt and thrive in the face of adversity. In the symphony of wellness, resilience serves as a refrain that strengthens your ability to achieve financial independence and personal flourishment. Developing resilience involves cultivating a positive mindset, building coping strategies, and seeking support when needed.

Start by embracing a growth mindset, which involves viewing challenges as opportunities for learning and growth. This perspective helps you navigate setbacks with optimism and determination. Practicing self-compassion and acknowledging your strengths and achievements also contribute to a resilient mindset.

Building coping strategies involves developing healthy habits and practices that support your well-being. This could include regular exercise, mindfulness, and engaging in activities that bring joy and fulfillment. Having a toolkit of coping strategies helps you manage stress and bounce back from setbacks.

Seeking support from your network of mentors, advisors, and loved ones is crucial during challenging times. Reaching out for help and guidance provides valuable perspectives and encouragement, helping you navigate difficult situations with greater ease.

Finally, maintaining a long-term perspective helps in building resilience.

Remember that setbacks and challenges are a natural part of the journey towards financial independence and personal flourishment. Staying focused on your goals and remaining adaptable in the face of change ensures that you continue to progress towards a harmonious and fulfilling life.

14

Chapter 14: The Opus of Legacy – Creating a Lasting Impact

Legacy is the lasting impact you leave on the world, and it is an integral part of the symphony of wellness. Creating a legacy involves not only achieving financial independence and personal flourishment but also making a positive difference in the lives of others and the world around you.

Begin by reflecting on the values and principles that guide your life. These core beliefs form the foundation of your legacy and influence the actions and decisions you make. Consider how you want to be remembered and the impact you wish to have on future generations.

Creating a legacy involves making intentional choices that align with your values and goals. This could include philanthropic endeavors, community involvement, and initiatives that promote positive change. Consider how your financial resources, skills, and experiences can be used to support causes and projects that matter to you.

Mentorship and education are powerful ways to create a lasting impact. Sharing your knowledge, experiences, and insights with others fosters growth and development in those around you. This could involve mentoring young professionals, teaching, or simply offering guidance and support to those in need.

Finally, documenting your legacy through an estate plan ensures that your wishes are honored and your assets are distributed according to your intentions. This plan should include provisions for charitable contributions, support for loved ones, and the preservation of your values and principles for future generations.

15

Chapter 15: The Finale – Celebrating the Journey

The finale of the symphony of wellness is a celebration of the journey towards financial independence and personal flourishment. It is a culmination of the efforts, achievements, and experiences that have shaped your life. Celebrating this journey involves acknowledging your successes, reflecting on your growth, and embracing the ongoing pursuit of balance and fulfillment.

Take time to celebrate your achievements and milestones along the way. Recognize the progress you have made towards your financial and personal goals, and appreciate the effort and dedication that have brought you to this point. Celebrating your successes reinforces your commitment to your goals and provides motivation for continued growth.

Reflect on the lessons learned and the experiences that have shaped your journey. Consider how challenges have contributed to your growth and resilience, and how your values and principles have guided your actions and decisions. This reflection provides valuable insights and reinforces the importance of staying true to your core beliefs.

The Wellness Symphony: Orchestrating Financial Independence with Personal Flourishment

In a world where financial stability often takes center stage, "The Wellness

Symphony" harmoniously combines the pursuit of financial independence with the nurturing of personal well-being. This book is a comprehensive guide that emphasizes the importance of balance, where financial growth and personal development work together to create a fulfilling life.

Throughout 15 engaging chapters, readers will embark on a journey that covers essential financial literacy, strategic planning, income maximization, and investment growth. The book delves into practical advice on debt management, wealth preservation, and the importance of building a strong support network. It also highlights the significance of mindfulness, generosity, resilience, and the creation of a lasting legacy.

"The Wellness Symphony" is not just about achieving financial goals; it's about integrating them with personal flourishment to create a holistic and harmonious life. By the end of this journey, readers will have a well-orchestrated plan to achieve financial independence while nurturing their overall well-being, leading to a life filled with purpose and fulfillment.